WISE QUOTES: ARISTOTLE

(150 ARISTOTLE QUOTES)

Rowan Stevens

A constitution is the arrangement of magistrates in a state.

A friend to all is a friend to none.

A great city is not to be confounded with a populous one.

A likely impossibility is always preferable to an unconvincing possibility.

A tyrant must put on the appearance of uncommon devotion to religion. Subjects are less apprehensive of illegal treatment from a ruler whom they consider god-fearing and pious. On the other hand, they do less easily move against him, believing that he has the gods on his side.

All human actions have one or more of these seven causes: chance, nature, compulsions, habit, reason, passion, desire.

All men by nature desire knowledge.

All virtue is summed up in dealing justly.

Anybody can become angry – that is easy, but to be angry with the right person and to the right degree and at the right time and for the right purpose, and in the right way – that is not within everybody's power and is not easy.

At his best, man is the noblest of all animals; separated from law and justice he is the worst.

Bad men are full of repentance.

Bashfulness is an ornament to youth, but a reproach to old age.

Both oligarch and tyrant mistrust the people, and therefore deprive them of their arms.

Change in all things is sweet.

Character may almost be called the most effective means of persuasion.

*Comedy aims at representing men as worse,
Tragedy as better than in actual life.*

*Courage is the first of human qualities because it is
the quality which guarantees the others.*

*Criticism is something we can avoid easily by
saying nothing, doing nothing, and being nothing.*

*Democracy arises out of the notion that those who
are equal in any respect are equal in all respects;
because men are equally free, they claim to be
absolutely equal.*

*Democracy is when the indigent, and not the men
of property, are the rulers.*

Different men seek after happiness in different ways and by different means, and so make for themselves different modes of life and forms of government.

Dignity does not consist in possessing honors, but in deserving them.

Each man judges well the things he knows.

Educating the mind without educating the heart is no education at all.

Education is an ornament in prosperity and a refuge in adversity.

Education is the best provision for old age.

Equality consists in the same treatment of similar persons.

Even when laws have been written down, they ought not always to remain unaltered.

Every rascal is not a thief, but every thief is a rascal.

Excellence is an art won by training and habituation. We do not act rightly because we have virtue or excellence, but we rather have those because we have acted rightly. We are what we repeatedly do. Excellence, then, is not an act but a habit.

Excellence is never an accident. It is always the result of high intention, sincere effort, and intelligent execution; it represents the wise choice of many alternatives – choice, not chance, determines your destiny.

Fear is pain arising from the anticipation of evil.

For what is the best choice, for each individual is the highest it is possible for him to achieve.

Friends hold a mirror up to each other; through that mirror they can see each other in ways that would not otherwise be accessible to them, and it is this mirroring that helps them improve themselves as persons.

Friendship is essentially a partnership.

Good habits formed at youth make all the difference.

Happiness depends upon ourselves.

Happiness is activity.

Happiness is an expression of the soul in considered actions.

Happiness is the settling of the soul into its most appropriate spot.

He who has never learned to obey cannot be a good commander.

He who is to be a good ruler must have first been ruled.

He who is unable to live in society, or who has no need because he is sufficient for himself, must be either a beast or a god.

Hope is a waking dream.

I count him braver who overcomes his desires than him who conquers his enemies; for the hardest victory is over self.

I have gained this by philosophy that I do without being commanded what others do only from fear of the law.

If liberty and equality, as is thought by some, are chiefly to be found in democracy, they will be best attained when all persons alike share in government to the utmost.

If one way be better than another, that you may be sure is nature's way.

In a democracy the poor will have more power than the rich, because there are more of them, and the will of the majority is supreme.

In all things of nature there is something of the marvelous.

In poverty and other misfortunes of life, true friends are a sure refuge. The young they keep out of mischief; to the old they are a comfort and aid in their weakness, and those in the prime of life they incite to noble deeds.

It is best to rise from life as from a banquet, neither thirsty nor drunken.

It is during our darkest moments that we must focus to see the light.

It is easy to perform a good action, but not easy to acquire a settled habit of performing such actions.

It is Homer who has chiefly taught other poets the art of telling lies skillfully.

It is just that we should be grateful, not only to those with whose views we may agree, but also to those who have expressed more superficial views; for these also contributed something, by developing before us the powers of thought.

It is not enough to win a war; it is more important to organize the peace.

It is not once nor twice but times without number that the same ideas make their appearance in the world.

It is possible to fail in many ways...while to succeed is possible only in one way.

It is the mark of an educated mind to be able to entertain a thought without accepting it.

It is unbecoming for young men to utter maxims.

It is well to be up before daybreak, for such habits contribute to health, wealth, and wisdom.

Knowing yourself is the beginning of all wisdom.

Liars when they speak the truth are not believed.

Love is composed of a single soul inhabiting two bodies.

Man is a goal seeking animal. His life only has meaning if he is reaching out and striving for his goals.

Man is by nature a political animal.

Men acquire particular quality by constantly acting in a particular way.

Men are swayed more by fear than by reverence.

Men create gods after their own image, not only with regard to their form but with regard to their mode of life.

Misfortune shows those who are not really friends.

Moral excellence comes about as a result of habit. We become just by doing just acts, temperate by doing temperate acts, brave by doing brave acts.

Most people would rather give than get affection.

My best friend is the man who in wishing me well wishes it for my sake.

No excellent soul is exempt from a mixture of madness.

No notice is taken of a little evil, but when it increases it strikes the eye.

No one would choose a friendless existence on condition of having all the other things in the world.

Obstinate people can be divided into the opinionated, the ignorant, and the boorish.

Of all the varieties of virtues, liberalism is the most beloved.

Perfect friendship is the friendship of men who are good, and alike in excellence.

Personal beauty is a greater recommendation than any letter of reference.

Persuasion is achieved by the speaker's personal character when the speech is so spoken as to make us think him credible. We believe good men more fully and more readily than others: this is true generally whatever the question is, and absolutely true where exact certainty is impossible and opinions are divided.

Piety requires us to honor truth above our friends.

Plato is dear to me, but dearer still is truth.

Pleasure in the job puts perfection in the work.

Poetry demands a man with a special gift for it, or else one with a touch of madness in him.

Poetry is finer and more philosophical than history; for poetry expresses the universal, and history only the particular.

Politicians also have no leisure, because they are always aiming at something beyond political life itself, power and glory, or happiness.

Poverty is the parent of revolution and crime.

Probable impossibilities are to be preferred to improbable possibilities.

Quality is not an act, it is a habit.

Republics decline into democracies and democracies degenerate into despotism.

Something is infinite if, taking it quantity by quantity, we can always take something outside.

Suffering becomes beautiful when anyone bears great calamities with cheerfulness, not through insensibility but through greatness of mind.

The actuality of thought is life.

The aim of art is to represent not the outward appearance of things, but their inward significance.

The aim of the wise is not to secure pleasure, but to avoid pain.

The antidote for fifty enemies is one friend.

The beauty of the soul shines out when a man bears with composure one heavy mischance after another, not because he does not feel them, but because he is a man of high and heroic temper.

The difference between a learned man and an ignorant one is the same as that between a living man and a corpse.

The duty of rhetoric is to deal with such matters as we deliberate upon without arts or systems to guide us, in the hearing of persons who cannot take in at a glance a complicated argument or follow a long chain of reasoning.

The educated differ from the uneducated as much as the living from the dead.

The end of labor is to gain leisure.

The energy of the mind is the essence of life.

The gods too are fond of a joke.

The greatest thing by far is to be a master of metaphor; it is the one thing that cannot be learned from others; and it is also a sign of genius, since a good metaphor implies an intuitive perception of the similarity of the dissimilar.

The happy life is regarded as a life in conformity with virtue. It is a life which involves effort and is not spent in amusement.

The ideal man bears the accidents of life with dignity and grace, making the best of circumstances.

The law is reason, free from passion.

The least initial deviation from the truth is multiplied later a thousandfold.

The moral virtues, then, are produced in us neither by nature nor against nature. Nature, indeed, prepares in us the ground for their reception, but their complete formation is the product of habit.

The most perfect political community is one in which the middle class is in control, and outnumbers both of the other classes.

The one exclusive sign of thorough knowledge is the power of teaching.

The roots of education are bitter, but the fruit is sweet.

The secret to humor is surprise.

The society that loses its grip on the past is in danger, for it produces men who know nothing but the present, and who are not aware that life had been, and could be, different from what it is.

The soul never thinks without a picture.

The true and the approximately true are apprehended by the same faculty; it may also be noted that men have a sufficient natural instinct for what is true, and usually do arrive at the truth. Hence the man who makes a good guess at truth is likely to make a good guess at probabilities.

The ultimate value of life depends upon awareness and the power of contemplation rather than upon mere survival.

The virtue of justice consists in moderation, as regulated by wisdom.

The whole is more than the sum of its parts.

The wise man does not expose himself needlessly to danger, since there are few things for which he cares sufficiently; but he is willing, in great crises, to give even his life - knowing that under certain conditions it is not worthwhile to live.

The worst form of inequality is to try to make unequal things equal.

There is no great genius without some touch of madness.

Those that know, do. Those that understand, teach.

Those who educate children well are more to be honored than they who produce them; for these only gave them life, those the art of living well.

Those who excel in virtue have the best right of all to rebel, but then they are of all men the least inclined to do so.

Through discipline comes freedom.

To be conscious that we are perceiving or thinking is to be conscious of our own existence.

To love someone is to identify with them.

To run away from trouble is a form of cowardice and, while it is true that the suicide braves death, he does it not for some noble object but to escape some ill.

To write well, express yourself like common people, but think like a wise man. Or, think as wise men do, but speak as the common people do.

We cannot learn without pain.

We live in deeds, not years; in thoughts, not breaths; in feelings, not in figures on a dial. We should count time by heart throbs. He most lives who thinks most, feels the noblest, acts the best.

We make war that we may live in peace.

We must be neither cowardly nor rash but courageous.

We must no more ask whether the soul and body are one than ask whether the wax and the figure impressed on it are one.

We praise a man who feels angry on the right grounds and against the right persons and also in the right manner at the right moment and for the right length of time.

Well begun is half done.

What it lies in our power to do, it lies in our power not to do.

What the statesman is most anxious to produce is a certain moral character in his fellow citizens, namely a disposition to virtue and the performance of virtuous actions.

Whosoever is delighted in solitude is either a wild beast or a god.

Why is it that all those who have become eminent in philosophy, politics, poetry, or the arts are clearly of an atrabilious temperament and some of them to such an extent as to be affected by diseases caused by black bile?

Wicked men obey from fear; good men, from love.

Wishing to be friends is quick work, but friendship is a slow-ripening fruit.

Wit is educated insolence.

Without friends no one would choose to live, though he had all other goods.

You will never do anything in the world without courage. It is the greatest quality of the mind next to honor.

Youth is easily deceived because it is quick to hope.

www.ingramcontent.com/pod-product-compliance
Lightning Source LLC
Chambersburg PA
CBHW071256070526
44583CB00017B/2497